blue eye dragon

blue eye dragon

TAIWANESE COOKING

JADE & MURIEL CHEN

瑞玉　　静芝

NEW HOLLAND

ACKNOWLEDGEMENTS

To Dad, for supporting me in all my adventures and teaching me invaluable lessons in life and in business.

To Melissa, for being the best Gu-Gu (Aunty) to Marcus, Xavier and Lucius.

For having my back with the restaurant and the kids

To Sri and Harry (David's Mum and Dad), for your understanding, patience, love and support.

To Chin-Ying (Aunty Michelle), for loving me like your own daughter.

For helping me even when I was too shy to ask for help.

To all the staff, for your hard work and dedication.

To the Blue Eye Dragon regulars; for loving our food and loyal support.

To the ladies and gentlemen who sponsored and/or attended our annual charity fundraisers;

thank you for digging deep for a good cause.

To Fiona and the team at New Holland for a fantastic job. Thank you for believing in Mum

and I enough for this wonderful opportunity—it's been an amazing experience.

DEDICATION

To Mum, Jui-Yù (Jade), who taught me everything from food, cooking, to life. I admire and respect you with all my heart. I hope one day I can be as good a mother as you.
To my Grandmother, Lùi-Mèi (below), who I was fortunate enough to have spent three years of my childhood with. To this day, I still think you cooked better than Mum. (Sorry Mum!)
To my husband, David, who loves and supports me unconditionally.
Thank you for our beautiful family.

六妹

FOREWORD BY JOHN NEWTON
EDITOR, *SYDNEY EATS*

The first time I ate Jade Chen's food served by her daughter Muriel I knew it was more than a one-night stand. This was to be a long drawn out affair. And so it has proven.

That first visit to their first restaurant, **grain, tea, rice & noodles**, was in 2004. I'm still going to their new restaurant, **blue eye dragon**, in 2008. And my family and I will continue to eat their food wherever they go. Why?

In my review of **grain**, I wrote: 'The food here sounds ordinary, but is made extraordinary by being so carefully and exquisitely made.' That's the secret—Jade's meticulous attention to detail in the selection of ingredients and execution of each dish. There is nothing sloppy or thrown together here. A Jade Chen *sanbei* (Taiwanese stir-fry) is, also as I wrote, 'a reminder that a properly made stir-fry is a thing of colourful beauty and culinary joy, the flavour of each vegetable distinct but united by judicious saucing' and not just a jumble of stuff thrown in a wok.

But food is only part of the equation in both the restaurant and this elegant book. Jade's daughter Muriel is the front of house spirit whose personality and deep sense of hospitality infuse whichever restaurant she is working in.

Between them, mother and daughter collaborate on food, its service and the room in which it is served. And that is how it is with this book.

Taiwanese food, as it was explained to me by Jade and Muriel (and Jade cooked in her own restaurant there for 25 years) is a selection of the best food from all over China. When Chinese Government forces fled the mainland to the island of Formosa (now Taiwan) in 1949 after their defeat by the communists, hundreds and thousands of people from all across China followed, bringing their regional cuisines with them. In the ensuing 50-odd years, Taiwanese has distilled into an interesting and eclectic cuisine in its own right. But the food you'll find in this book has passed through an additional filter: the culinary sensibility and inventiveness of Jade Chen.

When you begin to cook from its pages—and you will, it's a cook book you'll cook from, not leave languishing on the shelf—remember those two important parts of Jade's kitchen equation: selection of ingredients and execution of each dish.

Do not hesitate for a moment to take this book into your kitchen. Your friends and family will profit from your purchase.

CONTENTS

BLUE EYE DRAGON
MEALS AT HOME — MUM'S COOKING

Having a restaurant of my own has been a long-time dream since my teenage years. I guess it was because I was brought up in restaurants from the age of seven.

My Mum grew up in Yangmei in Taiwan. From the age of 13 my Mum learnt traditional Taiwanese cooking from my grandmother. She turned into such a good cook that after she married my dad, they decided to open a restaurant. They ran restaurants in Taiwan for about 25 years while I was growing up. The major influences in their cooking were from the Hakka and Hokkien regions in China where the family had their origins. Unlike many restaurants in Taiwan, the food was based on home-style food—they served traditional favourites but with some adjustments to make them unique. The restaurant was very successful.

I enjoyed every minute I helped out in their restaurants. I loved the interaction with customers, the rush and the fun. It was a challenge to get everything right every day.

I left my job in mid-2001—I needed to figure out my life and do some soul searching. To my surprise Tony, an acquaintance in real estate, gave me the contact details and location he thought would be perfect for a restaurant. I would not have opened **blue eye dragon** on the ground floor of the old Pyrmont Arms Hotel, if Tony had been involved in the lengthy contract negotiations. Tony is now a close friend.

Finally in September 2005 we opened. Every decoration in **blue eye dragon** means something special to our family. All the paintings in the restaurant are by aunty Jui-Zhen, Mum's eldest sister. The three-metre long calligraphy of the Chinese word for dragon was done by Mum's best friend's sister. The seven mini-statues were a gift from Mum's youngest sister, Jui-Ling in Los Angeles. The statue of Guan-Yin (Buddha) was a gift from Mum's youngest sister-in-law. The two wooden seats and the table with the dragon and phoenix were a gift from my third aunty almost 25 years ago. Mum and dad bought the statue of Dar-Mou (a martial arts Master) in Taiwan to guard the restaurant and Mum has collected all the teapots on the glass shelves over the last 20 years.

The food we serve at **blue eye dragon** is the food we eat at home. I hope you find the recipes easy to follow and quick to prepare at home for your family. 'If the food is not good enough to be on our dinner table, we don't serve it to our customers', my Mum always says.

When I was first asked to write this cookbook I was a little unsure whether anyone would be interested in Taiwanese cooking, or if our food at **blue eye dragon** is special enough to put in a book. But I know our food is special because all the recipes are Mum's recipes—her life's work.

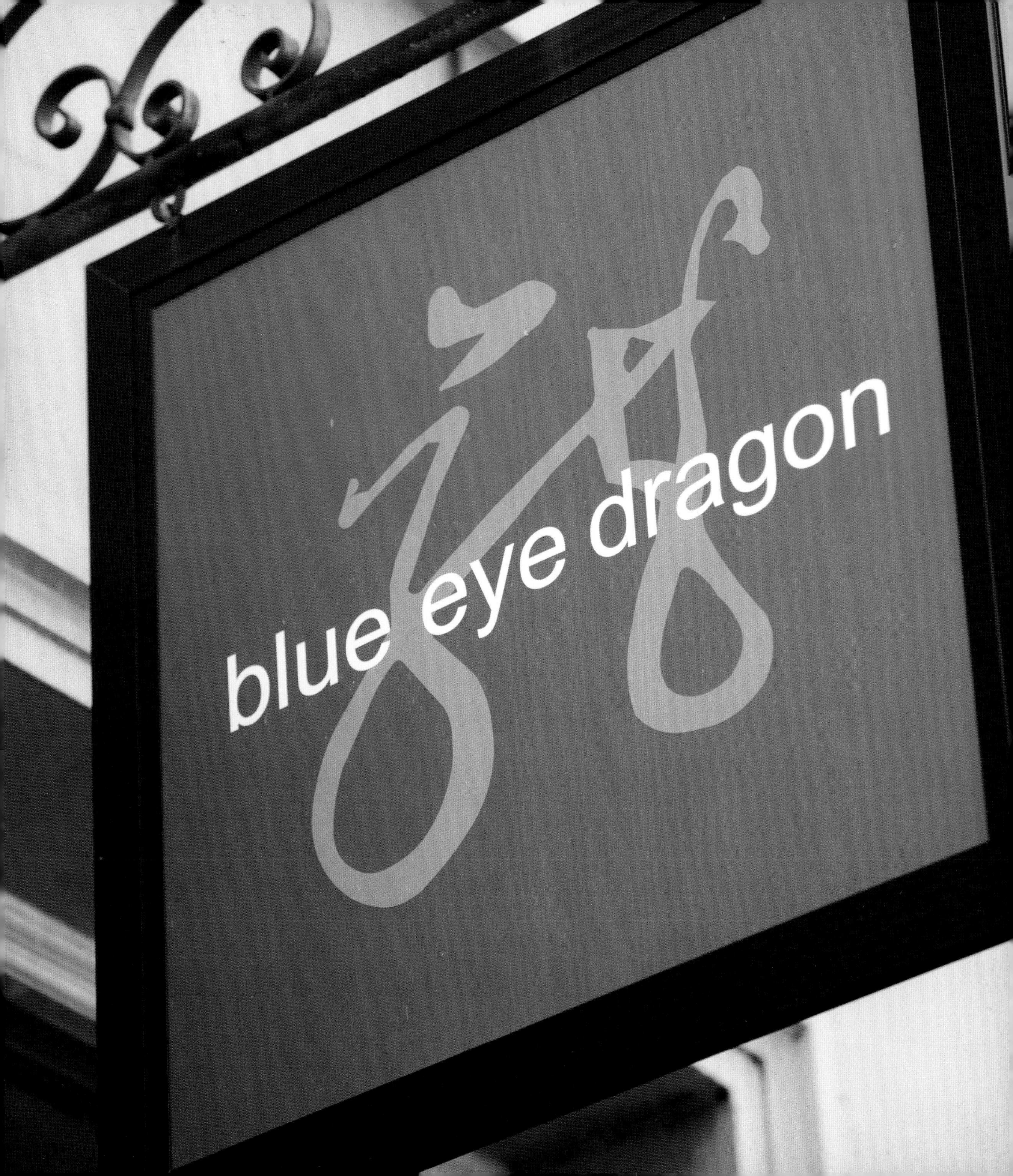
blue eye dragon

TAIWANESE FOOD: A BALANCE OF FLAVOURS

Customers often ask why our food is different from most Chinese restaurants and the answer is 'we are from Taiwan and, most importantly, they are my Mum's recipes'.

Most Taiwanese people are from China and our food is heavily influenced by Chinese cooking.

In addition to China's influence, Taiwan also has some Japanese flavours, as Japan occupied Taiwan for half a century after World War I. You'll often find Japanese dishes in Taiwanese restaurants, especially seafood restaurants.

Taiwan is probably most famous for its roadside food stalls rather than banquet dining. This style of food is the result of a highly competitive market, with small food business operators constantly needing to invent new flavours and dishes in order to survive.

Taiwanese cuisine is a mixing pot of good food from all over China and its use of local produce and creativity sets it apart from other Asian food. Blending together food from different provinces makes Taiwanese food a balance of all the flavours.

BASICS

In today's modern, busy life we tend to work longer hours and have less time for everything else. If you follow the basics in this section, cooking a meal for four people in 30 minutes will be easy. After each grocery shopping trip, Mum always takes the time to clean, cut and marinate everything, and only then stores them in the fridge or freezer. This means she can cook a meal for six of us in a very short time.

SERVING SIZES

All the stir-fry dishes make one serve only. All the entrée dishes are small, but can be doubled for a main dish. If you are cooking for more than one person, try not to double the quantities. Instead, either make a second amount separately or, even better, make a different dish and share! Mum always asks, 'How many people for dinner?', then she will always cook an extra dish. For example, for four people, she will always make five dishes.

Marinating should be very simple and easy, as you don't want to mask the natural flavours of the produce. One thing that's very important to us at **blue eye dragon** is the freshness and clean-cut taste of the food.

Storing the meat or seafood in serving quantity portions of around 250g (8oz) makes preparation quicker and less messy. For quick defrosting, pack each portion flat.

CHICKEN AND PORK

Whether it is chicken thigh or breast fillet, it is important to trim away the fat before cooking because this makes a difference to the taste. At **blue eye dragon** we use either 2cm (¾in) cubes or very thin 5cm (2ins) strips for stir-frying. With chicken, unlike beef or pork, you need to cut along the grain.

Pork is a beautiful *pink* meat that Asians love! Pork cheek is the best for stir-frying texture-wise, but it's hard to get. If you are concerned about fat, lean pork or pork loin are good. Pork is tougher than chicken so thinly slice against the grain.

To marinate 1kg (2lbs) of chicken or pork:
½ teaspoon salt
1 teaspoon sugar
2 tablespoons potato flour (see Glossary)
¼ cup water
2 tablespoons vegetable oil

Mix all the ingredients except the oil together using a lifting motion with your hands, until you can feel the water has been absorbed by the meat.

Add the vegetable oil and mix in.

Freeze in airtight containers in desired serving portions.

BEEF

At **blue eye dragon**, we use beef skirt steak for stir-frying. It is more expensive than the normal lean beef, but it is definitely worth the money. Make sure you cut against the grain, otherwise it will end up as chewy as beef jerky!

To marinate 1kg (2lbs) of beef:

1 teaspoon sugar
½ egg, beaten
2 tablespoons potato flour (see Glossary)
1 tablespoon soy sauce
½ cup water
2 tablespoons vegetable oil

NOTE: do not use salt if marinating beef

Mix all the ingredients except the oil together using a lifting motion with your hands, until you can feel the water has been absorbed by the meat.

Add the vegetable oil and mix in.

Freeze in airtight containers in desired serving portions.

PRAWNS AND FISH

To preserve freshness, peel and devein the prawns before marinating.

When freezing fresh (not peeled or marinated) prawns, it is best to freeze them in water.

To marinate 1kg (2lbs) of prawns:

¼ teaspoon salt
½ teaspoon sugar
3 tablespoons cornflour
ground white pepper, a pinch
1 egg white

Mix all the ingredients together and add to prawns. Freeze in airtight containers in desired serving portions.

Fish fillets should be cleaned and frozen in desired serving portions. If freezing a whole fish, make sure the fish is cleaned and gutted thoroughly. Then freeze in an airtight container.

STORING VEGETABLES

There is an old Chinese saying: 'Money knows quality'. This means the more expensive produce is expensive for a reason: it's the best. Of course, the best vegetables are always those in season. Vegetables are the hardest of the stir-fry ingredients to keep fresh, so Mum always purchases the best and spends time washing them and removing any yellow or loose leaves prior to storing them in airtight containers. This means we have coriander (cilantro) and basil in the restaurant that tastes as fresh as if they were just picked from the garden.

Mum frequently jokes that she treats the vegetables as well as she treats us; with lots of love and care.

DEEP-FRYING

At **blue eye dragon** we do all our deep-frying in a deep fryer so we can set the temperature just by using the dial. If you don't have a deep fryer then heat the oil in a wok. To test if it is at 180°C (350°F), the normal temperature for deep-frying, place a small cube of bread into the hot oil. If it browns within 1 minute it's hot enough.

STIR-FRYING IN A WOK

The main things to remember when stir-frying are to always to heat up the wok before adding the oil, and then make sure that it's very hot before beginning to stir-fry. Also you must never stir-fry large amounts, otherwise the results will be stewed. If you wish to make a larger portion try to make the dish twice, don't just double the quantities in one wok.

NOTE
To save freezer space, use cling film for each portion then place several packets in one airtight container.

WEIGHTS AND MEASURES

In this book we have used the following weights and measures:

Liquid measures

4 cups	1 litre	32fl oz	
2 cups	½ litre	16fl oz	1 pint
1 cup	250ml	8fl oz	
½ cup	125ml	4fl oz	
⅓ cup	80ml	2¾fl oz or 4 tablespoons	
¼ cup	60ml	2fl oz or 3 tablespoons	
1 tablespoon	20ml		
1 teaspoon	5ml		

Mass measures

1 kg	2lb
750g	1½lb
500g	1lb
300g	10oz
200g	6½oz
150g	5oz
60g	2oz
30g	1oz
15g	½oz
10g	⅓oz

XO Sauce

Caramelised
Kong-Bao Sauce

Dumpling Sauce
for Dumplings

Taiwanese Garlic
Five Spice Sauce

Garlic Chilli Sauce
with Chilli Beans

Fish Sauce

Sauces

Stir-frying is about balancing the beautiful flavours of all the ingredients—add too much sauce and the dish becomes stewed! Salt and sugar are normally enough for a light flavoured dish as the ingredients, blended together in a very hot wok, will become surprisingly tasty.

In Taiwan, most stir-frying does not involve lots of sauces; the most frequent and popular sauce my Mum uses is soy sauce and its quality determines how good a dish tastes.

Here are some ready-made bottled sauces that can be purchased in Asian grocery stores. They are a must for your pantry and are what we use at **blue eye dragon** (see page 195).

Kim Ve Wong Soy Sauce
Kim Lam Soy Paste
Kong Yang Black Vinegar
Kong Yang Rice Vinegar

In addition to these sauces, here is a list of the essential herbs and spices used throughout this book to make stir-fried food easy to make and tasty too.

Five spice powder
Ground white pepper
Garlic
Shallots (spring onions/scallions)
Ginger
Chilli
Coriander (cilantro)
Star anise

Chinese Dry Plums

Szechuan Peppercorns

Chinese Wolfberries

Licorice   Star Anise

Caramelised Kong-Bao Sauce

Part One
½ cup sugar
½ cup water

Part Two
1 teaspoon ground white pepper
½ cup sugar
2 pieces white rock sugar (see Glossary)
⅔ cup soy sauce
½ cup black vinegar (see Glossary)

1 tablespoon glutinous rice flour (see Glossary)

Part One

Cook the sugar with half of the water in a wok, the mixture will turn red in colour then dark brown.
Add the rest of the water and stir well.

Part Two

Add all Part Two ingredients. Bring to the boil.

Combine the rice flour with 1 tablespoon of water to make a paste.

Add the paste to the wok and stir well until sauce thickens.

Allow to cool before storing in bottles to refrigerate.

Makes 2 cups

Taiwanese Sweet and Sour Sauce

2½ tablespoons sugar
¼ tablespoon black vinegar (see Glossary)
½ teaspoon soy sauce
½ cup water
1 teaspoon potato flour (see Glossary)

Combine potato flour with 1 teaspoon of water to make a paste. Mix all the ingredients in a big pot, bring to the boil and stir in the paste to thicken the sauce.

Allow to cool before storing in bottles to refrigerate.

Makes 1 cup

Sweet and Sour Sauce

1 cup water
1 cup tomato sauce
1 cup sugar
1 cup rice vinegar (see Glossary)
¼ teaspoon preserved Chinese plum powder (optional—see Glossary)

Combine all ingredients and bring to the boil. Allow to cool before storing in bottles to refrigerate.

Makes 4 cups

Jade's Bloody Plum Sauce

¼ tablespoon preserved Chinese plum powder (see Glossary)
½ cup rice vinegar (see Glossary)
½ black vinegar (see Glossary)
½ tablespoon Worcestershire sauce
1 cup tomato sauce
½ tablespoon HP sauce (steak sauce)
2 cups sugar
chilli oil, a drizzle (see Glossary)
1 cup water

In a pot, bring water and all ingredients to the boil. Stir constantly. Allow to cool before storing in bottles to refrigerate.

Makes about 4 cups

Fish Sauce
blue eye dragon style

2 cups water
½ cup fish sauce
80g (2¾oz) white rock sugar (see Glossary)
3 slices dry licorice

In a pot, bring water and dry licorice to the boil. Add all ingredients, stir and bring back to the boil.
Remove the dry licorice. Allow to cool before storing in bottles refrigerate.

Makes 3 cups

Garlic Chilli Sauce
with Chilli Beans

500g (1lb) small hot chillies, finely chopped
300g (9½oz) garlic, minced
4 cups vegetable oil
¼ cup sesame oil
150g (5oz) chilli bean sauce (see Glossary)

Spread the chillies evenly over a large baking tray then sprinkle the garlic over the chillies.

Heat oil to 200°C (400°F) in a wok until almost smoking, then turn off the heat.

Use a large ladle to drizzle the hot oil all over the chillies and garlic, until all the garlic turns golden brown. Then stir the chillies and garlic together and continue to pour the hot oil over them.

Add the chilli beans sauce and sesame oil, then mix thoroughly. Allow to cool before storing in bottles to refrigerate.

Makes 6 cups

NOTE
To store the sauce in the fridge, make sure the chillies are fully covered in oil. If for any reason the oil is consumed faster than the chillies, add more sesame oil to cover.

Seafood Sauce (Hoi Sin Sauce)

2 tablespoons soy sauce
1 cup oyster sauce
⅓ cup rice wine
⅔ cup sugar

Mix all ingredients together on low heat. Stir through until sugar dissolves. Allow to cool before storing in bottles to refrigerate.

Makes 2 cups

Salt and Pepper

Bai-Chao
(Hundred Spices)

Curry Powder

Cinnamon

Ginger

Long chillies

Spinach

Chinese Celery

Garlic

Coriander

Basil

Shallots

Dipping Sauce for Dumplings

25ml (¾fl oz) chilli paste
75ml (2½ fl oz) soy sauce
1 teaspoon sesame oil
1 tablespoon vinegar

Mix all the ingredients. Store unused sauce in bottles to refrigerate.

Makes 100ml, enough for several servings.

032

Taiwanese Garlic Five Spice Sauce

This is great over squid, oysters and other seafood or as a barbecue marinade.

1 cup tomato sauce
¼ cup sugar
¼ cup soy paste (see Glossary)
¼ cup black vinegar (see Glossary)
1 teaspoon sesame oil
1 teaspoon chilli oil (see Glossary)
2 shallots (spring onions/scallions), finely chopped
10 slices ginger, finely chopped
5 cloves garlic, finely chopped
1 large red chilli, finely chopped or deseeded if required
1 small bunch coriander (cilantro), finely chopped

Combine tomato sauce, sugar, soy paste, vinegar, sesame oil and chilli oil, then stir until sugar has dissolved.

Add the shallots, ginger, garlic, chilli and coriander and mix well.

Makes 2 cups

NOTE
This makes a large quantity and unused sauce can be refrigerated in airtight bottles.

ENTRÉES, SIDE DISHES & CONDIMENTS

Deep-Fried Crumbed Chicken Fillets

2 chicken breast fillets
2 teaspoons salt and pepper mixture (see Salt and Pepper section)
½ teaspoon curry powder
2 eggs, lightly beaten
vegetable oil
2 cups cornflour
2 cups breadcrumbs

Trim each fillet into palm-sized pieces, making sure they are all the same thickness to ensure even cooking.

Combine a pinch of the salt and pepper mixture, curry powder and ½ tablespoon of the lightly beaten egg. Marinate the chicken and allow to rest for about 5 minutes.

Heat the oil in a deep fryer (or wok, see Basics) to 180°C (350°F).

On both sides, lightly dust the chicken fillets with the cornflour and then coat with the remaining beaten egg, before covering evenly with breadcrumbs.

Allow to stand for about a minute before deep-frying.

Once the chicken starts to float and turn golden brown they are cooked. Drain them on paper towels to absorb excess oil.

Cut the chicken fillets into long strips and serve with the remaining salt and pepper mixture on the side.

One serve

> **NOTE**
> Left over trimmed chicken pieces can be kept to make huntuns (wontons).

Crispy Chicken Wings

Marinade

2 cloves garlic, minced (ground)
1 teaspoon salt
1 teaspoon sugar
1 teaspoon curry powder
½ egg, lightly beaten
ground white pepper, a pinch
2 tablespoons cornflour
1kg (2lbs) chicken wings (about 12 wings, mid section only)
2 cups sweet potato flour (preferably crumbed–see Glossary)
1 tablespoon salt and pepper mixture (see Salt and Pepper section)
vegetable oil, for deep-frying

Combine the marinade ingredients and rub onto the chicken wings.

Heat the oil in a deep fryer (or wok, see Basics) to 180°C (350°F).

Coat the wings with the sweet potato flour, making sure they are well covered.

Allow to rest for about 1 minute.

Shake off any excess flour and place the wings in the deep fryer.

Once the chicken starts to float and turn golden brown they are cooked. Drain them on paper towels to absorb excess oil.

Sprinkle some of the salt and pepper mixture evenly over the chicken. Serve with the remaining salt and pepper mixture on the side.

One serve

Crispy Chicken with Basil and Five Spice

3 teaspoons salt and pepper mixture (see Salt and Pepper section)
½ teaspoon five spice powder (see Glossary)
salt, a pinch
sugar, a pinch
250g (8oz) chicken fillet, cut into 2 x 1cm (¾x½in) pieces
1 cup cornflour or sweet potato flour (see Glossary)
½ cup basil leaves

Combine the salt and pepper mixture and the five spice powder in a spice grinder or mortar until well blended. Set aside.

Marinate the chicken in a pinch of cornflour, salt and sugar and stand for a few minutes.

Heat the oil in a deep fryer (or wok, see Basics) to 180°C (350°F).

Lightly dust the chicken pieces with the remaining cornflour, then let them rest for about a minute before deep-frying.

Once the chicken pieces start to float and turn golden brown they are cooked. Drain them on paper towels to absorb excess oil.

Before putting the basil in the deep fryer, make sure you have the lid handy, as the basil will cause the oil to splatter. Fry the basil for 1 minute until crisp. Drain the basil.

In a big bowl, toss the chicken pieces with the basil and sprinkle with some of the salt and pepper and five spice mixture.

To serve, place the chicken on a plate, top with the basil and place remaining salt and pepper and five spice mixture on the side.

One serve

> **NOTE**
> Sweet potato flour gives a much crispier texture.

Chicken Roll with Water Chestnuts and Hundred Spices

200g chicken fillet, cut into long strips
1 teaspoon ground white pepper
2 tablespoons potato flour (see Glossary)
1 cup onion, diced
¾ cup water chestnuts (canned), diced
1 teaspoon Bai-Chao (Hundred Spices—see Glossary)
½ teaspoon five spice powder (see Glossary)

4 pieces bean curd pastry, 20cm (8ins) square (see Glossary)
1 teaspoon plain flour

Dipping Sauce

1 tablespoon chilli paste
1 tablespoon sweet chilli sauce

coriander (cilantro), to serve

Mix all the dry ingredients together with the onion.

Open up the bean curd pastry with the corner pointed towards you. Spread the onion mixture evenly to the centre of pastry, and then place chicken strips on top.

Combine the plain flour and 1 teaspoon of water to make a paste.

Roll up the pastry and seal the edges with the flour paste.

Heat the oil in a deep fryer (or wok, see Basics) to 180°C (350°F).

Fry the chicken roll until it floats then drain on paper towels to absorb excess oil.

Combine the chilli paste and sweet chilli sauce to make the dipping sauce.

Slice the roll with a sharp knife at an angle and serve with coriander and the dipping sauce.

One serve. Makes 4 rolls.

> **NOTE**
> Coriander is an absolute must for this dish as it really enhances the taste.

Chilli Chicken Huntuns (Wontons)

Filling

250g (8oz) minced (ground) chicken
salt, ground white pepper, sugar, a pinch
2 teaspoons potato flour (see Glossary)
1 tablespoon water

Sauces

1 teaspoon Garlic Chilli Sauce with Chilli Beans (see Sauces)
2 tablespoons Dumpling Sauce for Dumplings (see Sauces)

coriander (cilantro), to serve
1 packet huntun (wonton) pastry (see Glossary)
¼ lettuce, shredded, to serve

Mix together the filling ingredients until the water is absorbed into the chicken.

Place one teaspoon of chicken mince in the centre of a huntun pastry. Spread the mixture out over two-thirds of the pastry. Spreading out the filling means a pocket of air is left inside the pastry which makes them float.

Gather the edges of the pastry at the top. Pinch and twist to seal the top. Repeat with the rest of the pastry and mince.

Bring a large pot of water to the boil. Place the huntuns in the boiling water, stirring occasionally to avoid them from sticking to the pot. Once they float to the surface, wait a further two minutes, then drain them and put into a mixing bowl.

Stir in the sauces then serve the huntuns on top of the shredded lettuce. Garnish with coriander.

Makes two bowls of huntun.

> **NOTE**
> Huntun can be premade and frozen in airtight containers. Freeze them individually to shape before packing in a container.

Tea-Smoked Chicken

1kg (2lbs) chicken wings
2 litres (3½ pints) water
¼ cup ginger, sliced
2 shallots (spring onions/scallions)
½ tablespoon sugar
½ cup tea
1 tablespoon salt

048

Cut the wing part off the chicken pieces and just use the meaty part.

Bring the water to the boil in a big pot. Add ginger, shallots, salt and chicken wings. Bring back to the boil, then simmer for 15 minutes. Remove and drain wings.

Line a wok with foil. Spread the tea and sugar across the foil and place a mesh stand in the wok, then spread the chicken wings on the stand.

Place the wok over medium heat and cover with a lid to steam the chicken. When you can see 'yellow' smoke, turn off the heat and let it rest for 2-3 minutes, before you open the lid. The colour should be light brown. When the wings cool down the colour will darken.

One serve

> **Note**
> Traditionally in Taiwan we smoke the whole chicken. This recipe can be used with any part of the chicken or the whole chicken, with the skin on.

Drunken Chicken

1 tablespoon Chinese wolfberries (see Glossary)
4 chicken breast fillets
50g (2oz) ginger, thinly sliced
¼ cup salt
2 tablespoons sugar
2 shallots (spring onions/scallions), chopped

Marinade

1½ cups Shaoxing rice wine (see Glossary)
½ tablespoon salt
coriander (cilantro), to serve

Soften the wolfberries in water then dry on paper towels.

Bring some water to the boil in a pot, blanch the chicken quickly then remove from the water and drain.

Boil 4 more cups of water, then add in the ginger, salt, sugar, shallots and chicken fillets. Cover and cook for 12 minutes over low heat. Remove the chicken and keep the stock.

Combine 1½ cups of the chicken stock with the wine and salt.

Allow to cool before adding in the chicken and wolfberries.

Refrigerate for 24 hours.

Slice the chicken fillets to 1cm (½in) thickness and serve with some wolfberries and coriander. The remaining chicken stock can be used for soups.

One serve

NOTE
Breast fillet can be replaced with thigh fillet if preferred. If the fillet has the skin on, it will give a much better texture.

Prawn Spring Rolls

Filling

¼ teaspoon salt
¼ teaspoon sugar
1 tablespoon potato flour (see Glossary)
5½ tablespoons bonito powder (see Glossary)
600g (1¼lbs) prawns (shrimp), peeled, deveined and diced
100g (4oz) yellow chives, cut into 2cm (¾in) pieces (see Glossary)
30g (1oz) shallots (spring onions/scallions), finely chopped
160g (5oz) water chestnuts (canned), diced

1 tablespoon plain flour
30 sheets spring roll pastry (10cm/4ins size) (see Glossary)
1 piece nori paper, cut into ½cm (¼in) x 10cm (4ins) strips
vegetable oil
coriander (cilantro), to serve
2 tablespoons Plum Sauce (see Sauces)

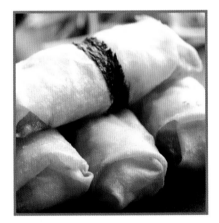

Combine all the filling ingredients except for the yellow chives and shallots. Then add the yellow chives and shallots and mix well.

Mix the plain flour with 1 tablespoon of water to make a paste.

Fill a spring roll pastry with a tablespoon of the mixture. Spread the mixture evenly over half of the pastry. Roll it up and seal with the flour paste.

Wrap a strip of nori around the centre of each roll, secure with flour paste.

Repeat with the remaining pastry and filling.

Heat up enough oil to deep-fry the rolls in a deep fryer (or wok, see Basics) to 180°C (350°F).

Fry the rolls until they start to float and are lightly brown. Drain on paper towels to remove excess oil.

Serve with some coriander and plum sauce on the side.

Makes 30

Spicy Chicken Wings
Caramelised in Soy Sauce

1kg chicken wings (10-12 wings), mid-section
5 garlic cloves, crushed, skin on
1 small red chilli, chopped (or left out if serving for children)
1 shallot (spring onions/scallions), cleaned, whole
½ teaspoons sugar
¼ cup soy sauce
½ cup water

To serve
sesame oil, to drizzle
cucumber slices, to garnish

Add all the ingredients in a wok and bring to the boil.

Simmer for 15 minutes and stir constantly. When cooked, turn on high heat to reduce the sauce and to caramelise. Drizzle with sesame oil and serve with cucumber slices.

One serve

> **NOTE**
> This dish tastes just as good when it is cool. You can also barbecue the cooked wings for a different taste, great for picnics in the summer.

Pork Dumplings

Filling

½ teaspoon salt
¾ teaspoon sugar
¾ teaspoon ground white pepper
1½ teaspoons ginger, minced
½ teaspoon soy sauce
⅓ cup water

500g (1lb) minced (ground) pork
150g (5oz) garlic chives, finely chopped
1 shallot (spring onions/scallions), green section only, finely chopped
2½ tablespoons potato flour (see Glossary)
sesame oil, a drizzle
dumpling pastry, 30-40 pieces (see Glossary)
Dipping Sauce for Dumplings (see Sauces)

Mix together all the filling ingredients until dissolved.

Add the mixture to the pork, using your hands to gradually mix together with a lifting motion until the water is absorbed.

In a separate bowl, mix the chives, shallots and potato flour together. Add this to the pork mixture and mix well. Finally, add the sesame oil and mix again.

Place 1 tablespoon of the pork filling in the centre of a piece of pastry. Dab around the edges with water. Fold the pastry together by pressing on the top edge of the pastry first, and then pleat the sides together to shape the dumpling.

Boil a large pot of water. Put the dumplings in the boiling water, stirring occasionally to avoid them from sticking. Turn down the heat once the water comes back to the boil. Dumplings should start to float after 4 minutes. Wait for another 2 minutes before removing them from the pot.

Serve with dipping sauce.

Alternatively, to pan-fry dumplings, place cooked dumplings on an oiled hot plate and fry until the bases of the dumplings are golden and crispy.

Makes 30-40 dumplings depending on filling sizes

NOTE
Fresh dumplings need to be left in the freezer on a tray, to shape and harden before being sealed in a container to store. Dumplings can be kept in the freezer for up to 2 months and take 2 minutes more than fresh dumplings to cook.

Prawn Dumplings

Filling

½ kg (1lbs) prawns (shrimp), peeled, deveined and diced
25g (1oz) Chinese celery, chopped finely (see Glossary)
75g (2½oz) shallots (spring onions/scallions), chopped finely
150g (9oz) water chestnuts (canned), diced
½ teaspoon ground white pepper

25g (1oz) potato flour (see Glossary)
1 bag of dumpling pastry (see Glossary)
Dipping Sauce for Dumplings (see Sauces)

Mix together all the filling ingredients and then stir through the potato flour.

Place 1 tablespoon of the filling in the centre of a piece of pastry. Dab around the edges with water. Fold the pastry together by pressing on the top edge of the pastry first, and then pleat the sides together to shape the dumpling.

Boil a large pot of water. Put the dumplings in the boiling water, stirring occasionally to avoid them sticking. Turn down the heat once the water comes back to the boil. Dumplings should start to float after 4 minutes. Wait for another 2 minutes before removing them from the pot.

Serve with dipping sauce.

Alternatively, to pan-fry dumplings, place cooked dumplings on an oiled hot plate and fry until the bases of the dumplings are golden and crispy.

Makes about 30 dumplings depending on filling size

> **NOTE**
> Fresh dumplings need to be left in the freezer on a tray, to shape and harden before being sealed in a container to store. Dumplings can be kept in the freezer for up to 2 months and take 2 minutes more than fresh dumplings to cook.

Stewed Beef Shin

2kg (4lbs) beef shin
1 tablespoon sesame oil to stir-fry

Spices

¼ cup ginger slices
10 whole cloves garlic, skin on
8 pieces star anise
1 teaspoon Szechuan peppercorns

Stewing Sauces

1½ cups soy sauce
6 cups water
1 tablespoon rice wine
2 tablespoons chilli bean sauce (see Glossary)
1 tablespoon sugar
1 shallot (spring onion/scallion)

To serve

1 shallot (spring onion/scallion)
sesame oil, a drizzle
stewed sauces, a drizzle

Wash the beef shin then bring a big pot of water to the boil. Put in the beef shin and cook for about 5 minutes. Drain.

Heat up the wok and stir-fry the spices with sesame oil until fragrant.

In a pot, put stewing sauces, beef and the stir-fried spices together. Bring to the boil and simmer for about 1½ hours over low heat with the lid on.

Remove beef from the pot and allow to cool to room temperature, then thinly slice.

Garnish with shallots and drizzle with some of the stewed sauces and sesame oil when serving.

One serve

> **NOTE**
> The remaining uncut beef shin can be stored in the freezer in airtight containers. Thaw in the fridge overnight before preparing to serve. The sauces can also be frozen.

Boiled Pork Belly
with Basil and Chilli Sauce

Dipping Sauce
5 basil leaves, finely chopped
1 chilli, finely chopped
2 tablespoons soy sauce

250g (8oz) pork belly
¼ cup ginger, finely shredded, to serve

Combine all ingredients for the dipping sauce.

Wash pork belly and clean the skin with a knife. Mum always says she's giving the pork a good shave!

Bring water to the boil in a wok, put in the pork belly and simmer for 20-30 minutes

Take out the pork belly, let it cool down to warm before thinly slicing.

Wash shredded ginger well in water to reduce the sharpness of the ginger taste.

Serve the sliced pork belly with the shredded ginger and dipping sauce.

One serve

> **NOTE**
> This is a beautiful dish—easy to make yet full of flavour.

Deep-Fried Prawns with Plum Sauce

1 egg white
salt and pepper mixture, a pinch (see Salt and Pepper section)
1 cup cornflour
10 tiger prawns (shrimp), peeled, deveined, tail left on
vegetable oil
Plum Sauce (see Sauces)

Mix together the egg white, salt and pepper mixture and 1 tablespoon of cornflour.

Combine with the prawns and leave to marinate.

Heat the oil in a deep fryer (or wok, see Basics) to 180°C (350°F).

Coat the prawns with the remaining cornflour in a tray. Let the prawns set for about a minute before deep-frying. Prawns are cooked when curled and floating.

Remove the prawns. Drain on paper towels to absorb excess oil before serving on a plate with the plum sauce.

One serve

> **NOTE**
> If plum sauce is not available, use sweet chilli sauce or salt and pepper mixture.

Scallops with Shallots and Fish Sauce

¼ cup Fish Sauce (see Sauces)
12 scallops, cleaned, roe on or off depending on your preference
1 shallot (spring onion/scallion), finely julienned
2 slices of carrot, finely julienned

Mix shallots and carrots together.

Heat up the fish sauce and keep warm.

Bring some water to the boil in a pot. Place the scallops gently in the water and cook for about 1 minute, until their colour changes to white. Quickly remove them from the pot and onto a serving plate.

Top scallops with shallots and carrots, then spoon the fish sauce over each one.

One serve

SALT AND PEPPER

Salt and Pepper Mixture

4 tablespoons salt
2 tablespoons sugar
1 tablespoon ground white pepper

Combine all ingredients in a spice grinder or mortar and pestle until well blended. When preparing large quantities, it is best to wok toss the salt over low heat to remove any excess moisture.

Makes more than half a cup

Note
Left over mixture can be stored in a well-sealed jar in a cool place (not refrigerated) for up to 3 months.

Salt and Pepper Squid

Salt and pepper dishes are very popular in Chinese and Taiwanese cuisine. There are several ways to do it. The process we use at **blue eye dragon** *is simple, but the crucial steps of wok tossing must be done exactly right to get a perfect result!*

Use as little oil as possible when tossing the shallots, garlic and chilli. You don't want any excess oil to be absorbed into the batter. A good trick is to use a spray vegetable oil, or rub a paper towel with a little oil on it over the wok.

1 whole squid
1 tablespoon salt and pepper mixture (see Salt and Pepper section)
vegetable oil, for deep-frying
1 cup cornflour
4-5 cloves garlic, finely sliced
1 long chilli, chopped (remove seeds if you want to minimise the spiciness)
2 shallots (spring onions/scallions), green section only, chopped

Clean the squid, cut the tubes open and cut a cross-hatch pattern into the insides. Be careful not to cut all the way through.

Cut the tubes into 4 x 2cm (2 x 1in) pieces and place in a mixing bowl with one pinch of the salt and pepper mixture, mix well.

Heat the oil in a deep fryer (or wok, see Basics) to 180°C (350°F).

Put the cornflour in a bowl and slowly add in enough water to make a batter with a consistency that is thicker than paint and slightly sticky. Then add in the squid. Use your whole hand to mix the squid with the batter, don't just coat the surface.

Slowly lower the squid into the hot oil, it should float when ready. Remove from the oil immediately.

Lightly oil a wok, place over high heat, throw in the garlic for a good stir and then the chilli and shallots. Finally add the squid, sprinkle with some of the salt and pepper mixture and give it all a good toss. Serve with some of the remaining mixture on the side.

One serve

Salt and Pepper Prawns

10 large fresh tiger prawns (shrimp), cleaned, deveined with tail on
1 tablespoon salt and pepper mixture (see Salt and Pepper section)
vegetable oil, for deep-frying
1 cup cornflour
4-5 cloves garlic, finely sliced
1 long chilli, chopped (remove seeds if you want to minimise the spiciness)
2 shallots (spring onions/scallions), green section only, chopped

080

Place the prawns in a mixing bowl with one pinch of the salt and pepper mixture, mix well.

Heat the oil in a deep fryer (or wok, see Basics) to 180°C (350°F).

Put cornflour a bowl and slowly add in enough water to make a batter with a consistency that is thicker than paint and slightly sticky. Then add in the prawns. Use your whole hand to mix the prawns with the batter, don't just coat the surface.

Slowly lower the prawns into the hot oil, they should float when ready. Remove from the oil immediately.

Lightly oil a wok, turn on high heat, throw in the garlic for a good stir, and then the chilli and shallots. Finally add the prawns, sprinkle with some of the salt and pepper mixture and give it all a good toss. Serve with the remaining salt and pepper mixture on the side.

One serve

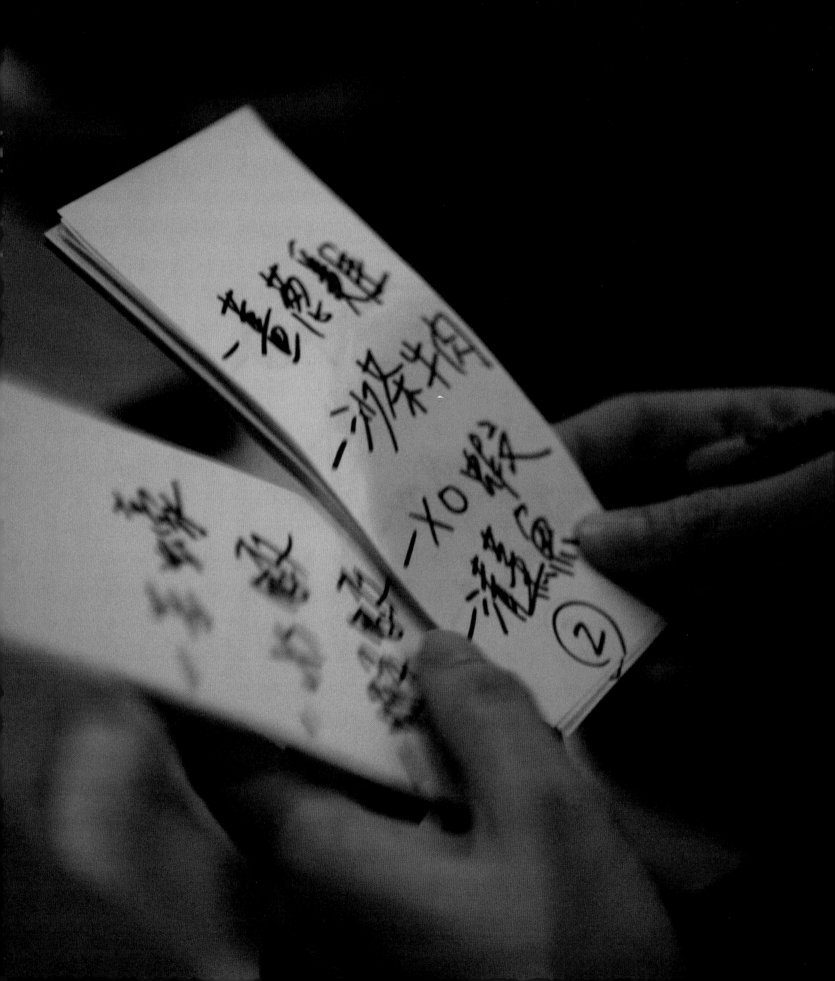

Salt and Pepper Soft Shell Crab

2 x 150g (5oz) soft shell crab
1 tablespoon salt and pepper mixture (see Salt and Pepper section)
vegetable oil, for deep-frying
1 cup cornflour
4-5 cloves garlic, finely sliced
1 long chilli, chopped (remove seeds if you want to minimise the spiciness)
2 shallots (spring onions/scallions), green section only, chopped

Clean and cut each crab into 6 pieces. Place the crab pieces in a mixing bowl with one pinch of the salt and pepper mixture, mix well.

Heat the oil in a deep fryer (or wok, see Basics) to 180°C (350°F).

Put cornflour in the bowl with the crab pieces. Coat the crab pieces well, allow to rest for a minute. Shake off excess flour before deep-frying.

Slowly lower the crab pieces into the hot oil, they should float when ready. Remove from the oil immediately.

Lightly oil a wok, turn on high heat, throw in the garlic for a good stir, and then the chilli and shallots. Finally add the crab, sprinkle with some of the salt and pepper mixture and give it all a good toss. Serve with the remaining salt and pepper mixture on the side.

One serve

Salt and Pepper Tofu

vegetable oil, for deep-frying
1 cup cornflour
tofu, cut into 4 pieces 1x10x2cm (½x4x¾ins)
4-5 cloves garlic, finely sliced
1 large chilli, deseeded and chopped
2 shallots (spring onions/scallions), chopped
½ tablespoon salt and pepper mixture (see Salt and Pepper section)

Heat the oil in a deep fryer (or wok, see Basics) to 180°C (350°F).

Put cornflour in a bowl and add the tofu. Gently coat the tofu and allow to rest for a minute.

Deep-fry until golden brown.

Lightly oil a wok, turn on high heat, throw in the garlic for a good stir, then the chilli and shallots.
Finally add the tofu, sprinkle with some of the salt and pepper mixture and give it all a good toss.
Serve with the remaining salt and pepper mixture on the side.

One serve

Salt and Pepper Whitebait

200g (6½oz) whitebait
1 tablespoon salt and pepper mixture (see Salt and Pepper section)
vegetable oil, for deep-frying
½ cup cornflour
4-5 cloves garlic, finely sliced
1 large chilli, deseeded and chopped
2 shallots (spring onions/scallions), chopped

Wash and drain the whitebait well. Mix the whitebait with the cornflour in a mixing bowl. Remove the whitebait and shake off excess flour.

Heat the oil in a deep fryer (or wok, see Basics) to 180°C (350°F).

Deep-fry the whitebait and drain on a paper towel.

Lightly oil a wok, turn on high heat, throw in the garlic for a good stir, then the chilli and shallots. Finally add the whitebait, sprinkle with some of the salt and pepper mixture and give it all a good toss. Serve with the remaining salt and pepper mixture on the side.

One serve

SOUPS

Chicken Noodle Soup
with Chinese Celery, Fried Shallots and Chinese Greens

1-2 stalks Chinese celery, finely chopped (see Glossary)
1 shallot, finely chopped
2 cups water (or chicken stock if available)
250g (8oz) chicken, cut into strips
2 cups egg noodles
1 teaspoon salt
2 drops soy sauce
1 teaspoon sugar
ground white pepper, a pinch
½ tablespoon fried shallots (see Glossary)
Chinese greens

In a large pot, cook the noodles and then use the same pot to blanch the Chinese greens. Drain until ready to use.

In another pot, bring hot water/stock to the boil and put the chicken strips in for a few minutes until cooked.

Place the noodles in a bowl, top with the remaining ingredients and pour in the chicken and stock/water—the heat will release the flavours.

Garnish with coriander.

One serve

> **NOTE**
> If Chinese celery is unavailable you can use Western celery, but it will not have as much flavour. Mum always keeps trimmed excess chicken pieces (not presentable enough for stir-fries) to make chicken stock. Bring water to the boil, add the chicken pieces and simmer for 10 minutes.

Chicken and Vegetable Soup with Egg Noodles

100g (4oz) chicken, cut into strips
2 tablespoons cornflour
vegetable oil, for deep-frying
2 cups egg noodles, cooked
2 Chinese mushrooms, soften in hot water and cut into strips
¼ cup carrot, shredded into strips
bamboo shoots
enoki mushrooms
200g (7oz) Chinese cabbage, cut into strips

Seasoning

1½ teaspoon salt
1 teaspoon bonito powder (see Glossary)
½ teaspoon sugar
½ tablespoon soy sauce
1 tablespoon black vinegar (see Glossary)
ground white pepper, a pinch
1 tablespoon potato flour mixed with 1 tablespoon water to make a paste (see Glossary)
coriander, (cilantro) to serve

Marinate chicken in the cornflour thoroughly. Heat oil in the wok and deep-fry the chicken until crispy. Drain on paper towels.

Bring 3 cups of water to the boil and add the vegetables. Bring back to the boil and add all seasoning and chicken. Thicken with potato paste.

Place noodles in a bowl and cover with the vegetable soup

One serve

> **NOTE**
> Replace chicken with pork if preferred. Traditionally in Taiwan, families use pork.

Chicken Huntun (Wonton) Soup

Filling

250g (8oz) minced chicken
sugar, salt and pepper, a pinch each
2 teaspoons potato flour (see Glossary)
1 tablespoon water
1 packet of huntun (wonton) pastry (see Glossary)

Soup seasoning

1 teaspoon salt
1 teaspoon sugar
ground white pepper, a pinch
2 drops soy sauce
1 shallot, finely chopped
½ tablespoon fried shallots (see Glossary)
1 stalk coriander (cilantro), chopped
Chinese greens
2 cups chicken stock/water

Mix the chicken with the salt, pepper, sugar, potato flour and water.

Stir until the water is absorbed into the chicken.

Place one teaspoon of chicken mince in the centre of a huntun pastry. Spread the mixture out over two-thirds of the pastry. Spreading out the filling means a pocket of air is left inside the pastry which makes them float.

Gather the edges of the pastry at the top. Pinch and twist to seal the top. Repeat with the rest of the pastry and mince.

Bring a pot of water to the boil.

Place the huntuns in the boiling water, stirring occasionally to avoid them sticking to the pot. Once they float to the surface, wait a further two minutes, then drain them and put into a serving bowl.

Use the same pot to blanch the Chinese greens. Drain and discard the water.

Boil the stock/water for the soup. Put all the soup seasoning over the huntuns in a bowl. Pour the soup over the huntuns and garnish with coriander.

One serve

Chicken Soup with Ginger, Wolfberries, Rice Wine and Sesame Oil

There is no water in this recipe at all. It is traditional in Taiwan to make this soup as an important daily meal, for a woman in the first month after she has given birth. It is believed that this will restore her to good health. It is full of nutrients and considered very warming—especially good if you feel cold and shivery!

500g (1lb) chicken thigh
1 tablespoon Chinese wolfberries (see Glossary)
¼ cup black sesame oil
50g (2oz) ginger, sliced
600ml (20fl oz) rice wine
salt, a pinch
½ tablespoon sugar

Cut chicken into 2-3cm (¼in) cubes.

Soak wolfberries in water to soften, then drain.

Heat wok over high heat. Add sesame oil and stir-fry the ginger until slightly dry and fragrant.

Toss in the chicken and stir-fry until almost cooked through.

Pour in half of the rice wine and bring to the boil. Be very careful as there is a danger of it catching fire—the rice wine is highly flammable.

Add the wolfberries and turn the heat down to medium, then add the other half of the rice wine.

Simmer for a few minutes until the chicken is fully cooked. Add the salt and sugar.

One serve

> **NOTE**
> Use the old woody type of ginger for this. In the old days, a whole chicken was used.

Taiwanese Traditional Beef Noodle Soup

This makes extra beef and stock. Freeze them separately and defrost them both when needed. Pour them over some noodles and you have a very quick and tasty meal.

2kg (4lbs) beef brisket
1 tablespoon sesame oil
¼ cup ginger, sliced
1 shallot (spring onion/scallion)
3 cloves garlic, minced
1 tablespoon star anise
3 teaspoons sugar
¼ tablespoon Szechuan peppercorns (see Glossary)
2 teaspoons chilli bean sauce (see Glossary)
15 cups water
1 tablespoon white rock sugar (see Glossary)

To serve

1 bunch spinach (silverbeet)
2 cups cooked white noodles
sesame oil, to drizzle
1 shallot (spring onion, scallion), finely chopped
1 stalk coriander
A few stalks of Chinese greens
chilli oil, to taste (optional—see Glossary)

Blanch the beef for 1 minute to make it easier to cut. Trim off most of the fat and cut it into 2cm (¾in) cubes.

Heat up the wok over high heat, add the sesame oil and stir-fry the ginger, garlic, star anise and Szechuan peppercorns until fragrant.

Add the sugar, chilli bean sauce, water and white rock sugar. Check at this point that it tastes a little bit salty. Add the beef.

Simmer for 80 minutes with the lid on. Remove beef and set aside. Sieve the liquid for the soup and reserve.

Blanch the Chinese greens. Place the noodles, Chinese greens and beef in a bowl and pour over enough soup to cover.

Drizzle with sesame oil, garnish with shallots and coriander or chilli oil to serve.

Combination Vegetable Soup with Crispy Fried Eggs

2 Chinese dried mushrooms
3 cups water
5 pieces (250g) Chinese cabbage, cut into strips
¼ cup enoki mushrooms
¼ cup carrots, cut into strips
1½ teaspoons salt
½ teaspoon sugar
1 teaspoon bonito powder (see Glossary)
½ cup vegetable oil
1 egg, lightly beaten
1 tablespoon potato flour mixed with 1 tablespoon water to make a paste (see Glossary)
2 cups egg noodles, cooked
coriander, to serve

Soften the dried mushrooms in a little water then drain, discard stalks and slice the caps into strips.

Heat the oil in a wok over high heat. Add the egg and stir with chopsticks in a circular motion until the egg is slightly set.

Lower the heat to medium—this is very important otherwise the egg will not cook through evenly. Slowly stir-fry until it smells like a cake and separates into strips.

Use the same wok and oil to quickly stir-fry the mushrooms until fragrant.

In a pot, bring water to the boil, add mushrooms, all the vegetables and seasoning, then bring back to the boil. Add the egg strips, stir quickly and mix in the flour paste to thicken.

Place noodles in a bowl and cover them with the soup.

Garnish with the coriander.

One serve

> **NOTE**
> Frying the crispy egg strips is the most crucial part of this recipe. Serve this dish a soup or together with the noodles.

MAINS

Pork Belly

2.5kg (5lbs) pork belly, skin on
400ml (13fl oz) soy sauce
2 shallots (spring onions/scallions)
5 cloves garlic, with skin off
3-4 pieces star anise
2 tablespoons sugar
½ tablespoon white rock sugar (see Glossary)
1 small chilli, whole
coriander (cilantro), to serve

Wash the pork belly and clean the skin with a knife. Mum always says she's giving the pork a good shave! Dry well with paper towels or a tea towel. Cut into 3cm (1in) cubes.

Spread the cubes out on an oven tray and place under the grill to quickly brown all sides. Traditionally, Mum would deep-fry the pork until golden but this can mean lots of wasted oil.

Put the pork belly and soy sauce in a large pan over high heat.

Stir thoroughly until the pork belly absorbs the soy sauce evenly (about 2 mintues). Then add enough water to just cover the meat, followed by the shallots, garlic, star anise, sugar and chilli.

Bring to the boil, then cook over medium heat—slightly higher than simmer, for 40-50 minutes without the lid on and stirring constantly.

For a softer texture, simmer for an extra 5 minutes, otherwise serve in a bowl and garnish with coriander.

Remove chilli and shallots before serving.

NOTE
This makes more than one serve. Freeze unused portions and reheat as required. Do not reduce the sauce too much, or it will be too salty.

Stir-fried Vermicelli with Pork, Vegetables, Dried Shrimp and Black Vinegar

3 dried Chinese mushrooms
1 tablespoon dried shrimp
¼ cup (60ml/2fl oz) vegetable oil
200g (7oz) pork, cut into thin 5cm (2ins) strips
1 cup onion, cut into strips
½ cup carrot, cut into strips
1 shallot (spring onion/scallion), cut to match the size of the carrot
2 leaves savoy cabbage, shredded (about 3 cups)
350g (11oz) cooked vermicelli, (100g (4oz) precooked)

Seasoning

ground white pepper, a pinch
2 tablespoons soy sauce
1 teaspoon sugar
1 teaspoon black vinegar (see Glossary)
¾ cup water
½ teaspoon salt

Soften the mushrooms in water. Drain, remove stalks and slice the caps. Soften the dried shrimp in water. Drain.

Heat up the wok over high heat. Add the oil, stir-fry the pork until almost cooked, then add the onion and stir-fry until soft. Add carrots, shallots, shrimp and cabbage and stir-fry for 1 minute.

Combine the seasoning ingredients and pour into the wok.

Lastly, add the cooked noodles and stir-fry on medium heat until they have absorbed the liquid, and taken on the colour of the seasoning. The noodle should taste a little bit chewy and elastic-like.

One serve

> **NOTE**
> Quality of the vermicelli determines how well this dish tastes.

Taiwanese Sweet and Sour Pork Ribs

350g (11oz) pork ribs, cut into 4-5cm (1½-2in) cubes
1 teaspoon soy sauce
sugar, a pinch
salt, a pinch
½ egg, lightly beaten
1 cup cornflour
vegetable oil, for deep frying
½ onion, cut into strips
2 tablespoons Taiwanese Sweet and Sour Sauce (see Sauces)
1 shallot (spring onion, scallion), washed and finely sliced/shredded, to garnish
1 long chilli, finely sliced/shredded, to garnish
vegetable oil, 1 tablespoon

Marinate the pork in the salt, sugar and egg for 10 minutes.

Place the cornflour in a bowl, add the pork and use your hands to make sure the pork is well coated.

Shake off excess flour and leave meat to rest.

Heat the oil in a deep fryer (or wok, see Basics) to 180°C (350°F). Add the pork a few pieces at a time and deep- fry for 3-4 minutes or until crispy.

As you remove each batch from the oil, drain it on paper towels.

Clean the wok, add 1 tablespoon of oil and lightly fry the onion until soft and fragrant.

Return the pork to the wok and add the Sweet and Sour Sauce, making sure all the ingredients are well coated. Garnish with finely sliced shredded shallots and chilli.

One serve

> **NOTE**
> Taiwanese sweet and sour sauce uses black vinegar which gives a different taste. Replace pork ribs with lean pork if preferred.

Stewed Beef Brisket with Spinach

2kg (4lbs) beef brisket
1 tablespoon sesame oil
¼ cup ginger, sliced
2 shallot (spring onion/scallion), whole
3 cloves garlic, minced
1 tablespoon star anise
3 teaspoons sugar
¼ tablespoon Szechuan peppercorns
2 teaspoons chilli bean sauce (see Glossary)
15 cups water
1 tablespoon white rock sugar (see Glossary)
1 bunch spinach (silverbeet)
½ tomato, cut into cubes
1 shallot (spring onion, scallion) cut into 2-3 cm (¾-1½ in) pieces
½ teaspoon potato flour (see Glossary)

Blanch the beef for 1 minute to make it easier to cut. Trim off most of the fat and cut it into 2cm (¾in) cubes.

Heat up the wok over high heat, add the sesame oil and stir-fry the ginger, garlic, star anise and Szechuan peppercorns until fragrant.

Add the sugar, shallots, chilli bean sauce, water and white rock sugar. Check at this point that it tastes a little bit salty. Add the beef.

Simmer for 80 minutes with the lid on.

Remove beef from the wok and set aside.

Sieve the liquid and reserve.

Combine potato flour with ½ teaspoon of water to make a paste.

In a separate wok, take ½ cup of the liquid, add tomato, shallots and 1 cup of beef. Add potato paste to thicken.

Blanch the spinach, drain well. Place spinach on a plate and spoon the beef and sauce over it.

One serve

> **NOTE**
> You can freeze the rest of the liquid and beef for later use in beef noodle soup.

Ginger Shallot Beef

250g (8oz) beef skirt, thinly sliced against the grain
1 tablespoon soy sauce
½ teaspoon sugar
potato flour, a pinch (see Glossary)
¼ cup (60ml/2fl oz) vegetable oil
½ cup ginger, thinly sliced
6 green shallots (spring onions/scallions), cut in 2–3cm (¾in) pieces
1 long chilli, thinly sliced at an angle

Marinate the beef with a drop of soy sauce, a drop of water, a pinch of sugar and potato flour. Mix well, then add a teaspoon of oil for a further mix.

Heat the wok to very hot before adding the remaining oil. Stir-fry the ginger until fragrant and then add the beef and quickly stir-fry.

Once the beef begins to change colour, add the shallots to the wok and stir. Finally, add the remaining soy sauce and sugar, mix through, remove from the heat and serve.

One serve

Beef in Taiwanese BBQ Sauce with Spinach

Marinade

1 teaspoon soy sauce
sugar, a pinch
1 teaspoon potato flour (see Glossary)
½ tablespoon water
1 tablespoon vegetable oil

250g (8oz) beef skirt
1½ tablespoons Taiwanese BBQ sauce (see Glossary)
250g (8oz) spinach (silverbeet), cut into 5cm (2ins) strips
2 tablespoons vegetable oil
2 cloves garlic, sliced
1 chilli, deseeded and cut at an angle
½ tablespoon soy sauce

Combine the marinade ingredients.

Thinly slice the beef against the grain and mix with the marinade for a few minutes.

Mix in the BBQ sauce.

Blanch spinach in water and drain.

Heat up the wok over high heat, add the oil and stir-fry the beef until almost done.

Add the garlic and chilli to the wok, stir then add in the soy sauce. Stir-fry until the meat is cooked.

Place the spinach on a plate and top with the beef to serve.

One serve

> **NOTE**
> Taiwanese BBQ sauce can be purchased from Asian grocery stores. Spinach can be replaced with other Chinese greens, such as water spinach or Chinese broccoli.

Chicken Fried Rice

150g (5oz) chicken breasts, cut into thin 5cm (2ins) strips
½ teaspoon salt
½ teaspoon sugar
1 teaspoon cornflour
2 tablespoons vegetable oil
2 cups steamed rice
2 eggs
¼ medium onion, diced
¼ medium carrot, diced and cooked
¼ cup diced shallot (spring onion/scallion), green end only
½ tablespoon soy sauce
ground white pepper, a pinch

To marinate the chicken, mix with a pinch of salt, sugar, cornflour, and some vegetable oil. Leave for 10 minutes.

Heat the wok to almost smoking, add some oil to moisten the wok, then add the eggs. Stir-fry the eggs until scrambled into pieces. Remove them from the wok when well done.

Use the same wok to stir-fry the chicken. When the chicken is almost cooked, add onions and carrots for a quick stir, then add the rice. Mix all together until the rice is heated through, then return the egg back to the wok.

Sprinkle the remaining salt, sugar and pepper over the rice and stir.

Drizzle with soy sauce and add chopped shallots for a final stir.

One serve

> **NOTE**
> Add ingredients to your liking, fried rice is all about what's available in the fridge. The most important part of the process is heating the wok before cooking. This will improve the texture of the fried eggs and the rice. The green end of shallots add colour to the fried rice.

Sanbei Chicken with Basil

250g (8oz) chicken fillet, cut in 2-3cm (¾in) cubes
¼ cup (60ml/2fl oz) sesame oil
¼ cup ginger, sliced
4 cloves garlic, sliced
2 shallots (spring onions/scallions), cut into 2cm (¾in) slices
1 chilli, chopped
2 tablespoons soy sauce
1 tablespoon soy paste (see Glossary)
2 tablespoons rice wine
2 tablespoons sugar
1 cup basil leaves

Heat up the wok over high heat, add the sesame oil and stir-fry the ginger for about 15-20 seconds.

Add the garlic and chicken to the wok and stir-fry until golden. Then add the shallots and chilli for a further stir.

Add soy sauce, paste, wine and sugar and stir-fry until the sauce is reduced.

Quickly stir through the basil then transfer to a plate and serve.

One serve

> **NOTE**
> If you have a cast iron bowl, heat up the bowl on the gas stove or in the oven to produce the sizzling effect when you serve. Traditionally in Taiwan, chicken maryland is used for this dish, and some use a whole chicken also.

Ginger Shallot Chicken

¼ cup (60ml/2fl oz) vegetable oil
½ cup ginger, cut into thin strips
250g (8oz) chicken, cut into thin 5cm (2ins) strips
6 green shallots (spring onions/scallions), cut in 2–3cm (¾in) pieces
½ teaspoon salt
½ teaspoon sugar
1 long chilli, thinly sliced at an angle (deseeded if you want to minimise the spiciness)

Heat the wok to very hot before adding the oil. Stir-fry the ginger until fragrant, then add the chicken and quickly stir-fry.

Once the chicken begins to change colour, add the shallots to the wok and stir. Finally, add the salt, sugar and chilli, mix through, remove from heat and serve.

One serve

Soy Paste Chicken with Shredded Shallots

250g (8oz) chicken, cut into thin 5cm (2ins) strips
½ teaspoon salt
½ teaspoon sugar
¼ cup (60ml/2fl oz) vegetable oil
2 tablespoons soy paste (see Glossary)

Topping

6 green shallots (spring onions/scallions), finely sliced
1 red chilli, deseeded and finely sliced

Marinate the chicken with the salt and sugar.

Wash the shallots and chilli after slicing to produce the curling effect, and to minimise the sharpness of the shallots.

Heat the wok to very hot and add the oil. Stir-fry the chicken until cooked through, then stir in soy paste and cook for a few seconds.

Transfer chicken onto a plate with shallots and chilli on top.

Mix together when serving at the table.

One serve

Chilli Curry Chicken

⅓ cup (80ml/2½fl oz) vegetable oil
250g (8oz) chicken, cut into cubes
½ onion, cut into bite-sized pieces
1½ tablespoons curry powder
3 snow peas
¼ cup capsicum (sweet pepper/bell pepper), cut into bite-sized pieces
1 chilli, chopped (add more if you life it hot)
¼ teaspoon salt
¾ teaspoon sugar
¼ cup water
1 teaspoon of potato flour (see Glossary)

Heat the wok over high heat and add the oil. Once hot, stir-fry the chicken until cooked, then remove from the wok.

In the same wok, stir-fry the onion until soft and fragrant, then add the curry powder and stir through.

Toss in the snow peas, capsicum, chilli, salt and sugar for a quick stir-fry before pouring in the water.

Combine the potato flour with 1 teaspoon of water to make a paste.

Once the sauce comes to the boil, stir in the potato paste to thicken then serve.

One serve

Chicken in Kong-Bao Sauce

250g (8oz) chicken, cut into 2–3cm (¾in) cubes

Marinade
salt, a pinch
sugar, a pinch
1 teaspoon vegetable oil

1 teaspoon potato flour (see Glossary)
¼ cup (60ml/2fl oz) vegetable oil
¼ cup ginger
¼ cup dried chillies
3 green shallots (spring onions/scallions), cut in 2–3cm (¾in) pieces
¼ cup Kong-Bao Sauce (see Sauces)

Mix the chicken with the salt and sugar, then when well combined mix in the oil.

Combine the potato flour with 1 teaspoon of water to make a paste.

Heat the wok over high heat then add the oil. When the oil is hot, add the chicken and quickly stir-fry until cooked. Remove from the wok.

In the same wok, add the ginger and stir-fry until fragrant, then add the dried chilli and shallots for a minute. Return the chicken to the wok and stir through the Kong-Bao sauce and serve.

One serve

Prawns in Jade's Bloody Plum Sauce

½ cup vegetable oil
25g dry vermicelli noodles/green bean noodle
8 large king prawns (shrimp), peeled and deveined, heads off and tails on
sugar, a pinch
ground white pepper, a pinch
1 tablespoon cornflour
vegetable oil for deep-frying
¼ cup (60ml/2fl oz) Plum Sauce (see Sauces)
salt, a pinch

Heat the wok over high heat, add the oil and fry the noodles until white and crispy. Drain them on paper towels and set aside to cool down.

Marinate the prawns in the sugar and pepper for a few minutes.

Coat the prawns in the cornflour, let it rest for a few minutes.

Heat the oil in a deep fryer (or wok, see Basics) to 180°C (350°F).

Fry the prawns in batches, when they float to the surface they're cooked. Remove them immediately and drain on paper towels.

Pour the plum sauce into a lightly oiled wok over high heat, return the prawns to the wok and toss well to coat evenly.

Serve the prawns on a bed of the deep-fried noodles.

One serve

Sweet and Sour Fish Fillets

250g (8oz) white fish fillets, cut in to 2x5x1cm (¾x2x½in) pieces
salt, a pinch
sugar, a pinch
½ egg, lightly beaten
1 cup cornflour
vegetable oil, for deep-frying
¼ onion, cut into 2cm (¾in) cubes
¼ red capsicum (sweet pepper/bell pepper), cut into 2cm (¾in) diamond-shaped strips
a few snowpeas
2 pineapple rings, cut to match the size of the capsicum
½ cup Sweet and Sour Sauce (see Sauces)

Marinate fish in the salt, sugar and egg for a few minutes.

Place the cornflour in a bowl, add the fish and use your hands to make sure the fish is well coated.

Shake off excess flour and leave to rest.

Heat the wok over high heat then add the oil. When the oil is hot, add the fish a few pieces at a time and deep-fry for 3-4 minutes till crispy.

As you remove each batch from the oil, drain it on paper towels.

Clean wok, add 1 tablespoon of oil and lightly fry the onion until soft and fragrant. Add in the snowpeas, capsicum and pineapple and stir.

Return the fish to the wok and add the Sweet and Sour Sauce making sure all the ingredients are well coated.

One serve

Pan-Fried Snapper with Ginger, Soy, Chilli and Shallots

1 whole 500g (1lb) snapper, cleaned
½ cup (125ml/4fl oz) vegetable oil
¼ cup ginger strips
2 shallots (spring onions/scallions), chopped
1 long chilli, cut at an angle
2 tablespoon soy sauce
1 tablespoon water
1 teaspoon sugar

Cut 3 slashes into the skin on each side of the snapper.

Heat the wok over high heat, add the oil and pan-fry the fish until golden brown on both sides.

Turn the heat to low and continue to cook the fish until tender—you can tell it's done if you can easily insert a chopstick into the flesh.

Push the fish to one side of the wok and stir-fry the ginger until softened, then toss in the shallots, chilli and soy sauce. Cook for a few seconds.

Turn the fish to coat it in the sauce, then add the water and sugar to finish.

Place the fish on a serving plate and pour over the sauce.

One serve

Sanbei Calamari with Basil

250g (8oz) calamari, cleaned, skin on and cut into 1cm (½in) rings
¼ cup ginger, sliced
2 tablespoons soy sauce
1 tablespoon soy paste (see Glossary)
2 tablespoons sugar
4 cloves garlic, sliced
2 shallots (spring onions/scallions), chopped into 2cm (¾in) slices
1 long chilli, chopped
¼ cup (60ml/2fl oz) sesame oil
2 tablespoons rice wine
1 cup basil leaves

Quickly blanch the calamari in a pot of boiling water—be careful not to overcook the calamari at this stage. Drain very well.

Heat the wok over high heat, add the oil and stir-fry the ginger until fragrant.

Add the garlic and calamari to the wok and stir-fry until golden. Then add the shallots and chilli for a further stir.

Add soy sauce, paste, wine and sugar and stir-fry until the sauce is reduced.

Quickly stir through the basil then transfer to a plate and serve.

One serve

> **Note**
> If you have a cast iron bowl, heat up the bowl on the gas stove or in the oven to produce the sizzling effect when you serve.

Scallops in XO Sauce

10 fresh scallops, roe and shell off
sugar, a pinch
cornflour, a pinch
1 teaspoon potato flour (see Glossary)
3 tablespoons vegetable oil
4 cloves garlic, sliced
2 shallots (spring onion/scallion), cut into 2-3cm (¾in) strips
1 long chilli, sliced at an angle
a few snow peas (mange tout/sugar peas)
¼ capsicum (sweet pepper/bell pepper) cut into diamond-shaped strips
2 tablespoons XO Sauce (see Glossary)
1 teaspoon sugar
1 teaspoon water

Marinate the scallops in a pinch of sugar and cornflour.

Combine the potato flour with 1 teaspoon of water to make a paste.

Heat the wok over high heat, add the oil and then stir-fry the scallops until they look plump. Remove from the wok.

In the same wok, stir-fry the garlic, shallots and chilli until fragrant, then add the snow peas and capsicums. Mix together, add the XO sauce, sugar and water and the return the scallops to the wok.

Stir in the potato paste to thicken the sauce then serve.

One serve

Ginger Shallot Calamari

350g (11oz) calamari, cleaned, skin on and cut into 1cm (½in) rings
1 teaspoon potato flour (see Glossary)
2 tablespoons vegetable oil
¼ cup ginger, cut into thin strips
6 shallots (spring onions/scallions), cut into 5cm (2ins) pieces
1 chilli, cut at an angle
½ teaspoon sugar
¼ teaspoon salt

Quickly blanch the calamari in a pot of boiling water—be careful not to overcook the calamari at this stage. Drain very well.

Combine the potato flour with 1 teaspoon of water to make a paste.

Heat the wok over high heat, add the oil and stir-fry the ginger until golden.

Add shallots and chilli and stir-fry.

Mix in the sugar and salt, then the calamari and stir in the potato paste to thicken the sauce.

Serve.

One serve

Seafood Congee

This recipe gives you a softer texture than a regular risotto. If you prefer to have your congee almost soup-like, add a bit more hot water before adding the seafood.

1 cup rice
9 cups water
ginger, few slices
1 small fish fillet, cut into 6 pieces
6 large green prawns (shrimp), deveined and halved
1 calamari, cleaned and cut into rings
6 scallops, roe off

Seasoning

1 teaspoon salt
1 teaspoon bonito powder (see Glossary)
ground white pepper, a pinch

2 shallots (spring onions/scallions), finely chopped
1 stick celery, finely chopped (or Chinese celery if available—see Glossary)

Wash rice well and drain.

Bring rice, water and ginger to the boil in a large pot, stirring constantly to avoid the rice from sticking to the pot. Once the water is boiled, turn the heat down to a simmer and cook the rice without a lid.

Meanwhile, use another pot of boiling water to blanch the seafood quickly. Drain.

Once the rice is cooked, and the water is significantly reduced, add the seafood and seasoning and bring back to the boil. Remove the pot from the heat.

Add the shallots and celery to the congee, mix well and serve.

One serve

> **NOTE**
> You can add any variety of seafood you like, just be careful not to overcook it.

Spicy Turban Shells with Garlic and Basil in Seafood Sauce

10 turban shells (should provide 1 cup of meat)
¼ cup vegetable oil
1 shallot (spring onion/scallion) cut into 2-3cm (¾-1in) pieces
1 clove garlic, minced
1 long chilli, sliced
2 tablespoons Seafood Sauce (see Sauces)
¼ cup basil leaves
sesame oil, to drizzle
2 iceberg lettuce cups

Bring a large pot of water to the boil and blanch the turban shells for about 1 minute. Drain and remove the meat from the shells, trimming off the hard part of the meat. Thinly slice.

Heat the wok over high heat, add the oil then the shallots, garlic and chilli. Stir well, then add the turban shell meat and Seafood Sauce and stir again briefly.

Add basil and sesame oil and mix thoroughly to finish.

Serve into two lettuce cups.

One serve

> **NOTE**
> Turban shells can be replaced with pipis or mussels (clams). Pipis need to be de-sanded in water before use. Both need to be quickly blanched before stir-frying.

Tofu stuffed with Minced Pork and Prawn in Black Pepper Sauce

Stuffing

250g (8oz) minced (ground) pork
60g (2oz) minced (ground) prawn
¼ shallot (spring onion/scallion), finely chopped
½ teaspoon Chinese celery, finely chopped (see Glossary)
ground white pepper, a pinch
sugar, a pinch
salt, a pinch
1 teaspoon sesame oil
½ tablespoon water
1 tablespoon potato flour (see Glossary)

10 pieces of tofu, cut into 3x5x1.5cm (1½x2x½in) pieces
¼ cup (60ml/2fl oz) vegetable oil, for deep-frying
¼ cup (125ml/4fl oz) soy paste (see Glossary)
black pepper, a pinch
½ teaspoon sugar
½ tablespoon water
10 shallots (spring onions/scallions), green part only
½ teaspoon potato flour

Combine the potato flour with ½ teaspoon of water to make paste.

Thoroughly combine the stuffing ingredients.

Make a hole in the middle of each piece of tofu and fill with the mixture. Pack as much into each one for a tight fit.

Steam over boiling water for 10 minutes. Let it cool before deep frying.

Heat the oil in a deep fryer (or wok, see Basics) to 180°C (350°F).

Deep-fry the tofu in batches, until crispy on the outside. Drain on paper towels.

Mix together the water, soy paste, black pepper and sugar, then add the tofu.

Bring the sauce to the boil then thicken with the potato paste. Serve on hot plate with shallots across to prevent the tofu from sticking on the plate.

One serve

Garlic Tofu
with Minced Chicken

2 cups vegetable oil, to fry tofu

1 tablespoon vegetable oil

tofu, cut in 2cm (¾in) cubes, do not use silken tofu or hard tofu

½ teaspoon potato flour (see Glossary)

¼ cup minced (ground) chicken

garlic, minced

1 chilli, chopped and deseeded

3 snow peas, cut into 2cm (¾in) pieces

3 button mushrooms, cut in half

1 carrot, a few slices

1 shallot (spring onion/scallion), finely chopped

Seasoning

5 tablespoons soy paste (see Glossary)

½ teaspoon sugar

ground white pepper, a pinch

sesame oil, to drizzle

Heat a wok over high heat. When it's hot, add the oil and deep-fry the tofu until crispy and golden in colour. Remove the tofu from the wok and discard the deep-frying oil.

Combine the potato flour with 1 teaspoon of water to make a paste.

Add 1 tablespoon oil to the still hot wok. Add the chicken, garlic and chilli and stir-fry for a few minutes. Stir in the snow peas and mushrooms before adding the seasoning.

Add tofu and shallots to the wok and mix well. Stir in the potato paste to thicken the sauce, then drizzle with the sesame oil and serve.

One serve

Chinese Turnip Omelette

4 eggs
2 tablespoons Chinese turnip, minced
¼ teaspoon salt
1 shallot (spring onion, scallion), finely chopped
½ teaspoon sugar
2 tablespoons vegetable oil
coriander (cilantro), to serve

Lightly beat the eggs and add all the remaining ingredients.

Heat the wok and add the oil. When it's very hot, add the egg mixture. Stir constantly until almost set then turn heat to medium. Use a spatula to shape the omelette. When golden, turn over and fry for a few minutes.

Garnish with coriander and serve.

One serve

Chinese Turnip Congee

1 cup rice
2 tablespoons dried shrimp
9 cups water
¼ cup (60ml/2fl oz) vegetable oil
150g (5oz) pork, minced (ground)
50g (2oz) Chinese turnip, finely chopped

Seasoning

1 teaspoon salt
1 teaspoon bonito powder (see Glossary)
ground white pepper, a pinch

2 shallots (spring onions/scallions), finely chopped
1 stick celery, finely chopped

Wash rice well and drain.

Soften the shrimp in water then drain.

Bring rice and water to the boil in a large pot, stirring constantly to avoid the rice from sticking to the pot. Once the water is boiled, turn the heat down to simmer and cook the rice without a lid.

While the rice cooks, heat the wok over high heat then add the oil.

Stir-fry the pork, turnip, shrimp and seasoning until fragrant.

Once the rice is cooked, add the turnip mixture and bring back to the boil. Remove the pot from the heat.

Add the shallots and celery to the congee, mix through well and serve.

One serve

Water Spinach with XO Sauce

Tossing Sauce

1 tablespoon XO Sauce (see Glossary)
½ teaspoon salt
1 teaspoon sugar
1 small chilli, thinly sliced at an angle
2-3 cloves garlic, sliced

400g (13oz) water spinach, cut in 2-3cm (¾in) pieces
2 tablespoons XO Sauce, to serve

Combine tossing sauce ingredients in a large bowl.

Boil a pan of water to blanch the water spinach, remove from the pan once the water comes back to the boil. Drain well.

Combine the spinach with the tossing sauce and mix well. Transfer to a plate and top with the remaining XO Sauce.

Serve.

One serve

> **NOTE**
> XO sauce can also be purchased ready-made from Asian grocery stores.

Stir-fried Chinese Cabbage with Crispy Egg Strips

300g (9½oz) Chinese cabbage
⅓ cup (80ml/2½fl oz) vegetable oil
1 egg
1 chilli, chopped
½ teaspoon salt
½ teaspoon sugar
½ teaspoon bonito powder (see Glossary)
1 teaspoon potato flour (see Glossary)

Cut Chinese cabbage leaves into chunks and the stems into finger-sized pieces for easy stir-frying.

Combine the potato flour with 1 teaspoon of water to make a paste.

Heat the oil in a wok over high heat. Add the egg and stir with chopsticks in a circular motion, until the egg is slightly set. Lower the heat to medium—this is very important otherwise the egg will not cook through evenly. Slowly stir-fry until it smells like baking a cake and separate into strips.

Remove the egg strips and leave the oil in the wok. Reheat until it's very hot, then stir-fry the cabbage until it reaches your desired texture. Add chilli, salt, sugar and bonito powder and mix through.

Return the egg strips to the wok for a final stir and mix in the potato paste to thicken the sauce.

One serve

Stir-fried Chinese Cabbage
with Bacon

Many of people would be surprised to see bacon in a Chinese dish. Before refrigeration in China, pork was preserved in salt and air-dried and called 'La Rou'. If you can find modern La Rou that would be great otherwise, like my Mum has done for over 20 years, you can just use bacon. This is one of my all-time favourite dishes; I could eat it everyday!

300g (9½oz) Chinese cabbage,
100g (5oz) of bacon rashes
1 teaspoon potato flour (see Glossary)
2 tablespoons vegetable oil
1 long red chilli, sliced into rings
¼ teaspoon salt
½ teaspoon sugar
1 teaspoon bonito powder (see Glossary)

Cut cabbage leaves into chunks and the stems into finger-sized pieces for easy stir-frying. For easier stir-frying, wash cabbage in hot water and drain very well.

Cut bacon into pieces the same size as the cabbage stems.

Combine the potato flour with 1 teaspoon of water to make a paste.

Heat the wok, add oil, heat it through and then add the bacon. Stir-fry until crisp or until it releases a lovely smell. Scoop into a bowl.

Put the cabbage in the same wok and quickly stir-fry. Once cabbage has softened, add the bacon, bonito powder, chilli, salt and sugar for a quick stir. Mix in the potato paste to thicken the sauce.

Serve.

One serve

Tomato Omelette with Chicken

2 medium tomatoes
1 teaspoon potato flour (see Glossary)
¼ cup vegetable oil
3-4 eggs
150g (5oz) chicken, cut into strips
1 teaspoon salt
2-3 teaspoons sugar
4 shallots (spring onions/scallions), chopped in 2-3cm (¾in) pieces

Cut across the top of the tomatoes and plunge into boiling water for a few minutes.

Remove from water, peel and cut into 2cm (¾in) cubes.

Combine the potato flour with 1 teaspoon of water to make a paste.

Heat half the oil in a wok over medium heat, lightly beat the eggs and pour them in.

Stir-fry eggs gently until they set into large-size chunks. Remove from wok.

Heat the rest of the oil in the wok and stir-fry the chicken until almost cooked. Stir in the tomatoes and shallots and cook for 1-2 minutes. Add the salt and sugar and return the egg for a quick stir.

Stir in the potato paste to thicken and serve.

One serve

DESSERTS

Sticky Rice with Wolfberries and Sultanas served with Sweet Peanut Powder and Coriander

2 cups sticky rice
2 tablespoons sugar
2 tablespoons Chinese wolfberries (see Glossary)
2 tablespoons sultanas
4 tablespoons sweet peanut powder (see Glossary)
1 stalk coriander, chopped

Soak the rice for 4 hours. Drain.

Place the rice in a steamer and poke holes through it with a chopstick to allow the steam to get through. Steam for 30 minutes.

When cooked, place in a bowl and stir in the sugar.

Mix the wolfberries and sultanas together.

Line 6 small bowls with cling film.

Place a spoon of the wolfberries and sultana mix in the bottom of each bowl and pack the rice in over the top—fill it well so it takes on the shape of the bowl.

Allow to cool to room temperature.

Invert each bowl onto a serving plate. Sprinkle the sweet peanut powder and chopped coriander around the dessert and serve.

Makes 6

NOTE
The rice can be frozen while in the bowls. It only takes 60 seconds in the microwave to defrost them for later use.

Sticky Rice Cakes in Ginger Syrup with Sweet Peanut Powder

My Mum always makes a large quantity of these and freezes them so we can have them as a treat any time.

½ kg (1lbs) glutinous rice flour
400 ml water
2 cups sugar
1 cup water
1 piece ginger (½ cup)
sweet peanut powder (see Glossary), to serve

Thinly slice the ginger and wash the slices. This preserves a good colour.

Boil the ginger, sugar and water until sugar dissolves.

Mix the flour and water together (it will be on the dry side similar to a scone mixture). Make one small patty from about one tenth of the mix and drop this into boiling water. When it floats and expands, take it out of the water and return it to the remaining flour and water mix.

Knead the patty back into the mix. The water it absorbed during cooking will be enough to moisten all the flour.

Knead well then roll and flatten into patties about 2cm-3½cm (¾-1½in) in diameter.

At this point the cakes can be frozen.

Drop them into boiling water in batches, cook for 6 minutes before removing from the water and draining.

Place the cakes on a plate, pour over the ginger syrup and add a few ginger slices. Top each rice cake with the sweet peanut powder and serve.

Makes enough for a party!

Sweet Red Bean
with Vanilla Ice-cream

500g (1lb) red beans
1½ cups sugar or to taste
⅓ cup potato flour mixed with ¼ cup water to make a paste
vanilla ice-cream, to serve
cocoa powder, to serve

Soak the red beans overnight to soften them.

The next day, bring them to the boil in about 10 cups of water.

Reduce the heat to very low and simmer for about 90 minutes or until the beans are soft.
Be careful not to cook them too fast or they will break apart or lose their skins.

Add the sugar to the pot and then the potato paste, which will soak up any remaining liquid
and thicken the red bean.

Chill.

Serve a scoop of red bean with ice-cream and dust with cocoa powder.

Serves enough for a party!

NOTE

Any cooked red bean that's left over can be frozen for future use. It can also be used to
make red bean soup. Just add hot water and sugar to taste.

Mum's love for tea

Mum's two favourite past times are cooking and making tea. I call her a tea-oholic. Why? She buys teapots and tea like sommeliers buy wine glasses and wine. Mum is addicted to her Dong Ding Oolong Tea. Dong Ding is a mountain in middle of Taiwan, famous for Oolong Tea because of its climate, soil and topography. Every year Mum will buy the same tea from the same tea-farmer's association.

It is an art to make Oolong Tea. Firstly, the water temperature needs to be 95°C (200°F). Tea leaves fill ¼ of the teapot, and hot water is added. The tea is brewed for about 60 seconds the first time. After the first pot is finished, add more water to brew again, but wait 70 seconds until the tea is poured. Add 10 more seconds for each successive brewing. The tea leaves are good for about six brews.

There are tea cups designed just for the aroma of the tea, and different tea cups for tasting. In addition to teapots and tea cups, tools for tea making include teaspoons, infuser, pincers, tea bowl, tea filter, tea boat and tea caddy. It takes minutes to just make one tiny cup of tea. Mum always tells me not to drink the tea that took her minutes to make in seconds, but to really taste, savour and enjoy it.

For over 20 years, Mum has been collecting teapots. Some of them are displayed at **blue eye dragon**. Oolong teapots are small; each brewing would just be enough for one round of tea for each drinker.

You could write a book about Oolong tea. No other type of shopping makes my Mum happier than tea and tea pot shopping. Mum's love for Oolong tea and teapots are indescribable.

GLOSSARY OF UNUSUAL INGREDIENTS

NOTE: Most ingredients listed below and throughout this book should be available in Asian grocery stores.

Bai-Chao (Hundred Spices): A combination of different herbs and spices. Frequently used in marinating, preserving, grilling and deep-frying. Generally very expensive and available in Chinese herbal stores.

Bean Curd Pastry: Is generally gluten free and made from yellow beans. Look for the thinnest pastry possible to give a much nicer texture when deep-frying.

Black Vinegar: Made from rice with fermented fruits and vegetables. Suitable for soups and noodles.

Bonito Flakes: Made from smoked bonito fish. They look like wood shavings. Commonly used in Japanese cooking.

Bonito Powder: A flavour enhancer made from smoked bonito fish.

Chilli Oil: Available ready-made in most Asian grocery stores.

Chilli Bean Sauce: Made from fermented soy beans with chilli and garlic. Widely used in Asian cooking and generally very salty.

Chinese Celery: Thinner and more fragrant than Western celery, the stems are longer and hollow. It is often mistaken for coriander and perfect for soups.

Chinese Wolfberries: Are orange-red, dried sultana-shaped Chinese herbs, also known as goji berries. Available in Chinese herbal stores and some Asian grocery stores.

Dumpling Pastry Wrappers: These wrappers are round and made from plain flour. Available from the refrigerator section in most Asian grocery stores.

Five Spice Powder: Available in Chinese herbal stores and Asian grocery stores. Quality varies according to herb and spices grading.

Fried Shallots: Made from red Asian shallots which are generally small in size. An essential topping ingredient in non soy sauce based soups.

Glutinous Rice Flour: Frequently used in Asian desserts to give more texture.

Huntun (Wonton) Pastry Wrappers: These thin, square wrappers are made from plain flour. They are available from the refrigerator section in most Asian grocery stores.

Potato Flour: A much better thickening agent, which gives a clearer and glossier finish than cornflour.

Preserved Chinese Plums: Are a popular Chinese snack food and available in powder also. Salty, sour and acidic in flavour.

Rice Vinegar: It should be made in a rice wine fermentation process, but generally is made from rice.

Shaoxing Rice Wine: A type of Chinese rice wine from Shaoxing County. Made from glutinous rice and wheat.

Soy paste: Much thicker than soy sauce. Not as strong in flavour as oyster sauce. Suitable for vegetarians.

Spring Roll Pastry Wrappers: Thin, elastic-like wheat based wrappers. Small, medium and large sizes are available from the refrigerator section in most Asian grocery stores.

Sweet Peanut Powder: Ground roasted peanuts mixed with castor sugar. The ration is generally 2:1.

Sweet Potato Flour: Also known as tapioca powder. It gives a much crunchier taste when deep-fried. Preferred in Taiwanese cooking and comes in a crumbed variety.

Szechuan Peppercorns: Look similar to black peppercorns and originally from Szechuan province in China. They give a much stronger aroma and flavour.

Taiwanese BBQ Sauce: Main ingredients include soybean oil, fish, garlic, spices, shallots, sesame oil, dried shrimp and chilli. Similar to what is commonly known as satay sauce.

White Rock Sugar: Are lumps of sugar which give food a cleaner taste. There is also a yellow-coloured variety available.

XO Sauce: Originated in Hong Kong in the 1980s. Main ingredients include dried scallops, dried shrimp and salted ham.

Yellow Chives: These are part of the Chinese chive family and have a lighter flavour. Generally not widely available.

Sauces you can find in your Asian grocery store.
Clockwise from left: Taiwanese barbecue sauce, soy sauce,
soy paste, black vinegar, Taiwanese rice wine and rice vinegar.

Thankyou to our customers:

Andrew & Tina, Peter & Pat, Richard & Shauna, Tony & Kim, Anthony & Linda, Fiona & Dave, Malcolm & Vicki, Peter & Helen, Robert & Helen, Phil & Jane, Drew & Lyn, Sue & Owen, Simon & Rebecca, Tim & Angie, Michael & Karie, Bill & Kerry, John & Kay, Stephen & Deborah, Peter H, Lily & Lawrence, Hank W, Glen & Nigel, Mat & Nigel, David & Chris, Dan & Giselle, John & Sue, Geoff & Maureen, Bruce & Barbara, Stan & Michelle, Ashley & Lindsey, David & Lyn, Rory Y, Mr & Mrs Winter, Mr & Mrs Morrisson, Irene & Maria, Adam L, Annette & Wentworth, Chris T, Gerard, Jacqui & Gavin, Jamie & Gavin, Mr & Mrs Beddington, Bruce, Paul & Donna, Sean & Michelle, Peter & Lyn, Pauline & Wayne, Roberta & Franz, Chris & Sharon, Strephyn & Tina, Rebecca A, the Craig family, Stefano M, John & De, Louise I, Kosta & Suzanne, Lily L, Margaret & Terry, Jim & Linda, John & Maureen, Dipsy A, Jason & Craig, Barry & Judith, Dushanka, Steve P, the Hannas, George I, Ron G, David P, Douglas H, Deirdre & David, Amelia C, Margaret M, Jim B, John B, Jeff, Graham B, John & Miriam, Gary M, David M, Adam A, Shane W, Shane P, Helen G, Ross & Mariet, Pamela R, Mike & Trish, John & Phillipa, Kim & Phillipa, Andrew & Lara, John & Suzanne, Peter R, Lucie T, Anette v K, Graham & Anne, Tony B, Roy & Maureen, Christine & Tony, the Wynyard family, Phil & Jackie, Ron & Terry, Gregory & Michelle, Doug & Sabine, John & Tennyson, Christine C, Don & Fran, the Jackson family, Donna, Adam, Alison & Marcus, Leticia, Trish & Antony, Sarah & Phil, Matt & Nigel, the Cheong family, Duncan & Angela, Michael, Sarah & Debbie W, Wendy, Carol S, Phil & Jane, Michelle, George I, Garth & Cindy, Garth, Peter & Margaret, Damien K, Anthony F, Cindy & Michael, Patrick D, Alex & Richard, Phillip & Davida, Gemma, Craig, Kevin, Susie, Virginia, Jenny, Helen & Ann, Ian B, Tracy, Ed, Sharon, Damien S, Ross, Frank & Maureen, Julian H, Brian H, Simon H, Zoltan, Marcelle & John, Neil, William W, Julie, Andrew, Geoff, Alan P, Malcolm, Justin, Susan K, Elizabeth, Deborah, Roger & Phoenix, Rebecca & Matt, Brad, Bill, Chantel, Danny, Grace, Jo, Ken, Kay, Darren, Marina K, Nicole, Nicholas, Ross M, Stephanie, Susie & Hargan, Tony, Antonio, Graham W, Mr & Mrs Freeman, Barbara, Louise, Denise & Harry, Lisa, Jenny & Matthew. Christine W, Douglas, Vanessa, The Nichollos, Peter H, Phil A, George & Maureen, Jessie, Ian & Gail, Gail, Mary & Don, Leonie, the Collins family, John B, Glen & Nigel, Walker & Web, Barry & Catherine, Tony & Sharon, Iari R, Kim D, Browyn & Michael, Arthur & Alicia, Paul & Claire, Chris G, Michael & Kim, Jacinta, Lisa L, Steven W, Jessie, Natalie, Catherine B, Warren E, Tea B, Helen W, Debbie S, Emma & Simon, Kim & Graham, Peter & Jacky, the Busby family, Max I, Christina T, Bianca, Naomi, Andy C, Mary M, Erin, David W, Rick & Sue, Ross P, Joe B, Wade S, Shelley, Phil & Simona, Dale, the Porter family, Val & Chris, Tempest, Rhonda, Mr. Bagshaw, Katerina, James R, Tim B, Jane R, Heidy, Mr & Mrs Booth, Adam O, Matt Q, Jennifer, Ellen, Ian S, John P, Chad & Lisa, Eddie & Deborah, Sylvia, Mark B

First published in Australia in 2008 by
New Holland Publishers (Australia) Pty Ltd
Sydney • Auckland • London • Cape Town

1/66 Gibbes Street Chatswood NSW 2067 Australia
218 Lake Road Northcote Auckland New Zealand
86 Edgware Road London W2 2EA United Kingdom
80 McKenzie Street Cape Town 8001 South Africa

A record of this book is held at the National Library of Australia
ISBN: 9781741106022

Publisher: Fiona Schultz
Publishing Manager: Lliane Clarke
Editor: Kay Proos
Proofreader: Melissa Sjahriar
Designer: Hayley Norman
Photography: Joe Filshie
Food stylists: Georgina Dolling and Carolyn Fienburg
Props supplied by Orson and Blake and The Bay Tree
Production Assistant: Liz Malcolm
Printer: SNP/Leefung Printing Co. Ltd (China)

10 9 8 7 6 5 4 3 2 1